10 Glam

COMMANDMENTS

GROW, LEVERAGE, ACCELERATE, AND MASTER BEING A WOMAN

To my Gidget, my I, my Kiddy cent. my amazing friend,

I Love You so much! Thanks for always being there

Lillie Ennis
Trumbull, Connecticut

Limits of Liability ~ Disclaimer
The author and publisher shall not be liable for your misuse of this material. This book is strictly for informational purposes. The author and publisher do not guarantee that anyone following the techniques, suggestions, tips, ideas, or strategies will become successful. The author and publisher shall have neither liability nor responsibility to anyone concerning any loss or damage caused, or alleged to be caused, directly or indirectly by the information contained in this book.

Book Coach – Robin Devonish
Cover Design – Nailah Morris
Formatting – Istvan Szabo, Ifj., Sapphire Guardian International

ISBN: 978-1-7338589-0-8

Printed in the United States of America

10 Glam
COMMANDMENTS
GROW, LEVERAGE, ACCELERATE, AND MASTER BEING A WOMAN

LILLIE ENNIS

I ACKNOWLEDGE...

This book was written at a very challenging time in my life and is dedicated to those who play a major role in my life and my success.

I must first thank the man above from whom all my blessings come from, Thank You, God!

Thank you to my parents and grandparents for my foundation. In life, whether good or bad, it made me who I am today. For my entire life, you have taught me to be strong and fearless. I appreciate you for that.

Thanks to my children, Omar and Landon, you are the reason why I eat, sleep, breathe and are my entire world. You are the reason why I can never keep a lid on my future. Your love stretches me to push further consistently.

Thanks to the amazing father of my children Oraine, I wouldn't be the entrepreneur that I am today had it not been for your influence.

Thank you my superhero Pastor, Apostle Cynthia G. West for the reminder, that no matter what I face the drama is for the fools. I am an A-lister that got paid sister. When I wanted to go low, you reminded me to go higher in God. You are such a blessing to my life.

Thanks to my mentors Johnny Wimbrey and Lucinda Cross who both instilled in me that I have several stories to tell. They both inspired me to be an amazing author.

Thank you, Robin Devonish, for assuring the success of this project since day one and holding my hand every step of the way.

Thanks to all my family and friends who have been there since day one. Your love and loyalty mean everything to me. Thank you for tolerating my craziness and all my ideas. There was the time we didn't speak, and there were holidays and celebrations that I missed, but your patience, love, and support mean everything to me.

I honor every woman that came into my life, best friend, friend, sister, family, mentor, and success partners, and I value you! It is our relationships that have shaped my experiences.

I DEDICATE THIS BOOK TO...

My amazing mother, Lilly Rosa aka Big Lil! Thank you for always being my rock and best friend. I want to thank you from the bottom of my heart for molding me into who I am today.

My pride and my joy sons, Omar Ennis and Landon Ennis, thank you for being my biggest inspirations to be the best version of me. I aspire to be the best mom on the planet because you are the best sons in the world.

TABLE OF CONTENTS

INTRODUCTION

Throughout my life, I've had this crazy unconventional relationship with my mom. My mother is less than five feet but boy when she enters a room does she command it. She will often greet you by saying, "Hi, my name is Big Lil!" At a whopping 4'11, she is a pillar of authority. In retrospect, I'm thankful that my first female role model was a strong one. However, I haven't always felt those sentiments.

When I was growing up, I loved sports. I was a big tomboy who preferred to dress, act, and sit like a boy because that's who I spent most of my time with. You would never see me hanging out with the girls and doing my hair or playing with makeup. You would see me playing basketball with the guys on "the block." I remember the good ole days when we would annoy the bodeguero (owner of the grocery store) and take his milk crates. Growing up in the Bronx, milk crates equaled three things, toys, basketball hoops, and seats.

I would rush home and finish my homework so I would have enough time to hang outside with my friends and play basketball. I utilized that time to socialize and wait until my mom came home from work and we would go upstairs and have dinner.

On one hot summer day, I was sitting in my basketball shorts on my crate waiting for my mom to arrive from work. Suddenly, I heard her scream at the top of her lungs, "Lillie close your fucking legs. I can see your ovaries." You may chuckle when reading this, but I remember being mortified. My face cheeks were on fire, my eyes became watery, and something within me changed. I became more aware that I was a young woman and started to own it. I began attending games dressed nicely, in skirts and then changing into my sports gear when it was game time.

The truth is, as raw and crushing the message was it was a defining and much needed moment for me. I could always count on my mother to be the person to tell me what I needed and not what I wanted to hear. From that day, I heard my mother's voice and wisdom more clearly. I am so glad our relationship has blossomed through the years because there were several lessons I learned from her as I entered adulthood. Had I not learned from her or been more open-minded to what she had to say, life would've been very hard. I thank God daily for her constant wise instruction. I know you are reading this Mommy my Mama Bear – I LOVE YOU!!!

I know that being a woman is filled with life challenges. Sometimes we reach crossroads and don't know which way to go. Everyone wants that cool big sister that's going to look out and keep it real. I am writing this book in hopes that you, dear reader, will gain value and clarity should you find yourself at a crossroads. I pray that this book will have the same effect on you as my mother's rawness had on me. I pray this book will provide you some gems that I know will enhance your life. I now present to you:

THE 10 GLAM COMMANDMENTS

COMMANDMENT ONE
THOU SHALL LOVE YOURSELF

What is love? For women that one word can be defined in different ways. Some say love is a feeling. Some may say love is the absence of hurt. Some will argue that a person who truly loves you isn't capable of hurting you. Others will correlate love to how you feel about someone else. My question for you is what does it truly mean to love yourself?

I feel, to truly love yourself, you have to do so unapologetically. Sometimes loving on you can be a scary thing because of the many backlashes from others. The minute a woman is encouraged to love herself you will hear commentary such as:

"Oh, she's a feminist."
"Oh, she's vain."
"Oh, she's selfish."

Over the years women have been conditioned to be nurturers. We're instinctively taught to take care of everyone else but ourselves. Often adult women are typically responsible for:

- taking care of spouses
- taking care of children
- taking care of elderly parents
- taking care of siblings
- taking care of close friends

Who takes care of you? Who loves you? We give so much of ourselves and give and give and give until our cup is empty. When does the giving cup get refilled? We look to receive the love we give. Our hearts get crushed when that same effort, attention, and love isn't reciprocated. Ladies you have to advocate for yourself! There is a spirit of love and confidence you must own and operate in. Experience taught me that haters will whisper your success and have the audacity to shout your failures. You can be on a roll, it's your year. You can be a super mom, a great friend, a wonderful wife. Or, someone in business having an explosive year and very few people will acknowledge you. It's challenging for people to congratulate others in their winning season. Let's say in that same winning season you hit a hurdle or a detour, maybe just a slight snafu - Honeyyyyyyy you have now made the news. Social Media will have a field day with your challenge.

What I just shared happened to me first hand. In 2014, my oldest son, who happens to be an entrepreneur, had a banner year. He was able to succeed not only in business but balance academics and athleticism. One day we sat down, and he mapped out an idea for an awesome youth empowerment conference. We were so excited because the idea had never been done in our city. We felt the youth truly needed this type of event and exposure. We hired a keynote speaker, printed flyers and promoted hard on social media. There was much effort to make the event a huge success. As the big day drew near, we were crushed because the response, support or sharing wasn't there. A week before the day we made an executive decision to cancel the event due to low registration. I remember posting the cancellation, and you wouldn't believe what happened next. The cancellation flyer received over fifty shares on Facebook, but the initial flyer only received two. Although the situation infuriated me, it was a great learning point.

I learned:

1. Toot my own horn regardless of what happens.
2. I must love and believe in myself through ups and downs.
3. I must stand firm in confidence.
4. No one will love or support me more than me supporting myself.

LILLIE-ISM

"When Confidence Is Met
With Insecurity, They Call It
Arrogance."

My favorite part about being a woman is motherhood. As a mom, and if you're a mom you can agree, we go through mommy or wife guilt. If someone or something is pulling us away from those two areas, we tend to feel bad. However, I want to know who wrote the book that said if you are a mom or a wife, you're a martyr. Why should a woman decrease for the ones she loves to increase? I have seen many women lay everything down because a spouse got a promotion or a child decided to play a new sport or try a new activity. Now don't get me wrong, I believe sacrifice to be an honorable and admirable thing; however, it must be a two-way street.

In my line of business, countless women have ceased chasing their dreams and goals because of lack of support from home. There were times where I've personally felt like a bad mother because I went days without seeing my children. I have had to work on their birthdays and holidays. Missing special moments was truly heartbreaking for me.

Let me offer some perspective. If a man does this, he is considered a hero, a provider, and is cheered on. On the flipside if a woman takes these actions she is considered neglectful, she is also oppressed. Why is it that being a good wife or a mom is equated with not being able to take a season for yourself? Why is it taboo to put yourself first so that you can reach a goal?

It saddens me especially when we are working for our families. If you don't put yourself first, you will never be happy because you are living to please others.

In this chapter I come against the spirit of lack in loving yourself; I come against the spirit of feeling you are not enough. If no one has told you, you are a bad mamma jamma; you are one of a kind. There is something so innate and incomparable that God hand selected you to do something that no one else can. I am Omar and Landon's mommy, and I know that is part of my superpower. We all must walk in our purpose and uniqueness. The biggest mistake I've seen a woman make was to allow the thief, called comparison, to creep in. I've never once wanted to be a model; nevertheless, I have always wanted to be a mogul. That alone is me operating in my purpose.

Many women are obsessed with following, but, not the right things. Who cares if you don't have the biggest boobs or butt? Do you have a big heart or a big wallet? Time out for seeking social media validation and checking to see how many people like you. Rather, ask yourself do you like you. Are you willing to be unpopular if the trade-off is pure happiness?

I promise you, your death bed the discussion will not cover how many likes were accrued. The personal question and introspect discussion will be (1) Did I love myself? (2) Did I live my best life for me? Don't be the person that knows what you love about everyone else but you did not know what you loved about you.

```
┌─────────────────────────────────────────┐
│                LILLIE-ISM                │
│                                          │
│  "You Are Your Biggest Preacher, Make    │
│   Sure You Tell Yourself How You Are     │
│              Loved Daily."               │
└─────────────────────────────────────────┘
```

Homework time! A mentor of mine had me do this assignment a couple of years ago, and I could not believe how hard it was for me to complete.

If you asked me to list three things that I love about my children, it would be challenging for me to narrow down all I love about them in three statements.

If you also asked me to list three things that I loved about my mother or any other loved one, I would have the same response.

Your assignment? Write three things you love about yourself. Then, I need your help to complete this part in changing the narrative on Social Media. Post those three things on social media and hashtag. #10GLAMLOVE

THOU SHALL LOVE YOURSELF
WORKSHEET

Name three things you love about yourself:

-
-
-

"When We Learn To Love Ourselves, We Stop Putting
Our Self-Esteem In The Hands Of Others."

A Compliment To Myself:

"The Strongest Actions For A Woman Is To Love Herself,
Be Herself, and Shine Among Those Who Never Believed
She Could."

What's Unique About Me?

-
-
-

What Do I Love About My Body?

●

●

●

What Can I Do To Strengthen My Mind?

●

●

●

"When I Accept Myself, I Am Freed From
The Burden Of Needing The World To Accept Me."

COMMANDMENT TWO
THOU SHALL FORGIVE YOUR PAST

One day I was having a character building moment. The words 'stressed out' were an understatement. I remember looking online to take my mind off of my situation, and I saw a quote that honestly resonated with me. The quote read, "Don't judge me by my past. I don't live there anymore." That quote rang loud in my spirit. I began to think and question my patterns and realized that I'm too hard on myself. I'm the type of person who doesn't need anyone to beat me down because I do it all to myself. What I found even odder is that half of the things I was punishing myself for were from the past. I had to take a moment, do some self-talk and forgive myself for the times I messed up. I learned that forgiveness is not just about forgiving others but about growing and forgiving yourself.

LILLIE-ISM

"I Am Not Who I Was!"

There is so much power in that statement because life is all about growth; however, society has a way of trying to punish you for growing. I was raised in very humble beginnings. My hometown is none other than The Boogie Down Bronx, NYC. I recall attending college in Connecticut and being surrounded by diversity. It was my first time being around not just different ethnicities such as Blacks, Latino, Asians, and Caucasians, but it was amazing meeting students from different American states such as Kentucky or Iowa. I was truly amazed and excited to be in college. While attending Sacred Heart University, I also enrolled in the international program where I made friends from India, Portugal, Spain, Hungary, Canada, and the list goes on.

I was ecstatic about my first Thanksgiving break from college because I missed all my neighborhood friends so much. It was nostalgic and exciting to go home and talk to them about my experiences at the university. I was walking around and singing a country music song that my college roommate jammed to all the time. I received an earful from my neighborhood friends. They kept saying things like:

"Why are you talking like that?"
"You switching up on us?"
"Oh, you are using big words now!"

I quickly realized not much had changed since I left for school. What was the result of not changing? Bitterness! As I continued to visit home after several college breaks the conversations with that specific group of friends were always directed to, "Remember when we did this? Remember when we went here?"

I learned this type of behavior was very common. Don't be the person that is so in love with their past that you wear it like a badge of honor and have nothing current to discuss. People will allow their past to dominate them. They love talking so much about whom they were that they don't create an identity for now. Let's be real ladies we have all heard the stories- "Oh in High School I used to run a seven-minute mile." "Oh in college I used to dance the night away." "Oh, back in the day, I was sharp."

LILLIE-ISM

"Your Past Is So Comfortable, Cluttered, and Crowded That You Forgot To Make Room For The Future."

It saddens me to see how many people allow themselves to be paralyzed by their past. It's time to stop being a cry baby! People will declare what they don't or won't do and justify it because of their past. I have heard it all, "I don't exercise because I have asthma." "I don't allow my child to go to theme parks because I witnessed a roller coaster get stuck." Now I know what you're thinking, who the hell does she think she is talking to me like that? I understand completely. It's like my mentor Johnny Wimbrey says, "When I'm talking to you I'm talking to me too!"

During the winter when my oldest son was three years old, unfortunately, I was in two bad car accidents. Both times someone hit me in the snow and kept driving. One of the accidents was so bad that the front and the back of the car were totally detached. It looked like someone crumpled a piece of paper on both ends. My son and I escaped without one single scrape. When I saw what the car looked like I vomited. I couldn't believe I came out of that situation unharmed. I vowed that I would never drive in the snow again. This would be difficult considering I live in the state of Connecticut where it's not uncommon for it to snow about eight inches. Sometimes in the month of May there are still signs of snow.

As I continued to grow and work on myself, I learned that I could not serve two masters. Faith and fear cannot occupy the same space. I began to speak life into my fears and situations.

I faced things head on and began to run toward what I was running from.

One of my favorite scriptures says that death and life lie in the power of the tongue. Instead of attracting what I didn't want to happen to me, I started to declare victories all around me. I would say things like, "Thank You God for the traveling mercies you are bestowing upon me today." I would also declare things like, "Thank You Universe for orchestrating this safe journey for me today." Once I stopped letting the fear of my past control me I was able to create a better future for myself by increasing my level of awareness.

> **LILLIE-ISM**
>
> "Don't Become So Obsessed With TBT
> (Throwback Thursday) That You Don't
> Have A Future."

What I hope will comfort you is what I call the 3 P's

- Problems
- Produce
- Purpose

Perspective is everything. Having problems or dealing with your past isn't always bad; it often indicates areas of growth. Accepting challenges will cause you to produce. What does it mean to produce? Don't complicate it, to produce simply means to take action. Don't dwell on a thing; act on it. Once you take action toward your past, it will produce purpose. Problems are always a good indicator of where you are headed.

When I was in college, I wanted nothing more than to be a physical therapist. I was passionate about reforming health care in an innovative way and be the best healthcare professional there was. After a couple of years working in the hospital, I was diagnosed with Breast Cancer. Talk about having a huge problem on my hands. I went into action and started to produce. I sprang into being proactive and decided to fight this disease differently.

What I didn't realize was that battling cancer would give me so much purpose. Shortly after being diagnosed

I lost my place of employment. That was one of those, 'when it rains it pours' moments. For a short while I was upset with myself for getting sick. I've always been driven and being sick put a wrench in my life's plans. I know I didn't have any control of that moment but still had a hard time forgiving myself. As I look back to that point in my life, all I can do is smile because my past produced purpose. I am healed, I have forgiven myself, and God has enlarged my territory and gave me a new platform to help people.

LILLIE-ISM

"Allow Your Difficulty To Become Your
Development; Your Experience To Be
An Educator And Your Test Be Your
Testimony."

THOU SHALL FORGIVE YOURSELF
WORKSHEET

Name three things from your past that are holding you back from your future:

●

●

●

Name three people in your life who you draw strength from:

●

●

●

I am becoming a great problem solver because:

_____

_____

_____

_____

_____

_____

_____

_____

"Life Is Tough My Darling, But So Are You!"

COMMANDMENT THREE
THOU SHALL BE COMMITTED

Nowadays, commitment is a huge word that many shy away from. I'm not talking about romantic relationships only. There are many avenues where commitment is a huge issue within people's lives. Whether business, personal, hobby or employment, commitment is the word that mends between where you are and where you want to be.

Every year the months January through April are tight for me, in a good way. It is the busiest season for all of my businesses. I was thinking of writing this book for a long time but decided to commit, even in my busiest season, to drop my first book ever during Women's History Month in March. Although it was stressful, I lost a lot of sleep, and had multiple deadlines, but I stayed committed.

I learned that unless there is a commitment, there are only promises and hope. Commitment and sacrifice go hand in hand. When you fall in love with what you are, being committed to the sacrifice will never seem bad. My pastor always says, "Saying your committed is not enough; the evidence must be present." Where is your proof? The evidence will hold you accountable.

LILLIE-ISM

"The Biggest Commitment You Can Make Is To Become The Best Version Of You."

Commitment can be tricky. One must know what they are committed to. Are you committed to your pride, your excuses, and your downfall? Or are you committed to your progress, your goals, and your results? The problem is that we live in a microwave society where people expect success to be easy or instant. People do things for a benefit or an outcome. When the outcome doesn't manifest fast enough, many tend to give up. You might run across this scenario where you may get the desired outcome, and quickly lose it as fast as obtaining it. Would you commit to getting it back? This happens more often than you think. If you are playing on a sports team and you are taking a hit – do you stop? Or are you the person to come back with a vengeance? If you are a soldier at war and it seems you are losing the battle – do you retreat? Or do you stand your ground and stay committed long after the feeling is gone?

LILLIE-ISM

"Your Life Will Only Change When You Become More Committed To Your Goals Than You Are To Your Comfort Zone!"

Keeping the end in mind will help you stay committed. The moment you set out to commit to a goal, detours are guaranteed to be in your journey. Coming across any setbacks and crossroads, forces you to make decisions, being mindful, of the decision. Will it bring you one step closer to your goal or one step further away?

For example, I am a huge food lover. I love dining out and trying varied restaurants. I am also a big fan of desserts. At the time of writing this book, the years' personal goal and commitment was to lose 20 pounds and to cut out sugars. Both my sons have birthdays in February, and of course, there was cake, soda and all kinds of goodies at their celebrations. However, I had to think with the end in mind. If I cheat and eat this one slice of cake will I have the will power to stay off the sweets? Will eating the goodies bring me closer to my goal or further away? Because I stood firm in that mindset I was able to meet my goal.

Having a strong why is a key ingredient in the decision-making process. Your why is your motivating factor toward a dream or a goal. I was taught that a good way to figure out your why is to ask yourself, "WHAT HURTS YOU?" There is something in all of us that keeps us up at night. There is a strong purpose that wakes you up in the morning. When you identify that, ladies you have found your why. You will hear women say that they want to eat healthier, or they want to go back to school, perhaps they want to start a business, and the list goes on.

The minute you declare a goal, it will feel like the universe is conspiring against you. It's quite ironic! I'm pretty sure you have experienced it for yourself, the one day you set out to impress your boss and go in early to get work done there is traffic. It's like making oatmeal for breakfast and taking it to work and forgetting to bring a spoon. Life will test you, but you cannot forget about your commitment. It baffles me when I coach my mentees they will say they are working on a goal because:

- They want to win at life simply because they are tired of losing
- They want to help a spouse out with the bills at home
- They want to give their children a better life
- They want to retire their parents
- They want to improve their quality of life

However the minute they go through any hardship they decide to call it quits. Giving up is a huge indicator that either you're a liar or your "WHY" was never strong enough. If keeping the end in mind, there is no way all those reasons I just listed are less important than any hardship you're facing. It's not supposed to be easy; if it were easy, then everyone would have it. The goals are not designed to be easy, but it is supposed to be worth it. When life attacks you, that's when your commitment level must increase to match the attack.

Battling cancer had to be one of the most challenging experiences in my life. Once you go through something you think will kill you, every day after that is a gift. My "WHY" became my children. I wanted to generate an income from home so that I can spend as many moments with them as possible. I also wanted to make sure, God forbid, if that hideous monster ever tries to come for me again, my children were well taken care of. I wanted to ensure that their quality of life went uninterrupted. So when people are mean or don't support me, that cannot stop my commitment goals because my sons are more important than anyone's NO. I remind myself to let that fuel me and keep pushing.

There was a point in time while building my network marketing business I was close to reaching a significant level. If I reached the level of Regional Marketing Director, I would receive a huge promotion. Not only would it benefit financially and in lifestyle, but allow me to take my family on our dream vacation. Once I achieved this rank in time, I would receive recognition at the next big event, on a huge stage, in front of thousands. I vividly remember sitting my boys down and explaining to them that I was going on a serious run and was taking the next 90 days to meet this goal. As I pursued, it would probably be hard on them because mommy wouldn't be around as much. I explained to them the sacrifices necessary to take part in on both our ends. I also elaborated on how sweet the victory would be when the goal was completed. Let's say that everything that could've gone wrong in that season did! On the morning of the deadline to meet my goal, I landed in the hospital with pneumonia. I wasn't taking good care of myself. I had a bad cold and breathing issue. Instead of recuperating and resting I was getting in front of the room doing presentation after presentation. The average person would have given up but my "WHY" was too strong.

What a lot of people didn't know is, although the goal seemed far away I had promised my children that I was going to do this. I had promised them that they would walk the big stage with me at recognition. And to seal the promise, I purchased their flights to come with me. We picked out our outfits and I envisioned the moment for so long that I refused to be a liar to them. I had to be a woman of my word and not let them see me fail at my goal. I got up when I could barely breathe, and I made phone call after phone call and made eleven sales to hit my goals because I was COMMITTED no matter what or who got in my way.

LILLIE- ISM

"If You Don't Sacrifice For What You Want, What You Don't Want Becomes The Sacrifice."

That lesson was so important for me because, in life, people will never follow what you say but will follow what you do. Based on that experience my children learned to be disciplined, committed, and to take risks. They learned that nothing ventured means nothing gained.

I hope that this level of resiliency and commitment is a reminder that you truly can accomplish anything you desire. Although things may seem like it's not working out in your favor, it is bringing out a higher dimension of you.

THOU SHALL STAY COMMITTED WORKSHEET

WHAT YOU DESIRE	IDEAL ACTIONS	CURRENT ACTIONS	UPDATED COMMITMENT

"Be all in or get all out. There is no halfway!"

COMMANDMENT FOUR
THOU SHALL BUILD A BRAND

It is no secret that I am a multiple business owner and serial entrepreneur. In business, you will see two words tend to pop up a lot – Marketing and Branding. Marketing is the strategy of how you promote and sell a product or service. A brand speaks for you; it is who you are when you enter a room. Branding is how you communicate to the public or your audience. The reason why I state the importance of a brand is because whether you are a businesswoman or not everyone has a brand. Before my being in business, my sister Zulli would walk past a store and say I just saw a shirt with huge ruffles, it's so Lillie. That is a brand.

A brand is a Blueprint.
It creates a united theme that translates consistently across all arenas of your message. It helps to build trust and loyalty towards your brand.

A brand is a Relationship.
It is a strong merger of who you are and why you exist? What is your purpose? What do you say about yourself? If you are servicing a problem, how are you the solution? Does the relationship component also entail what your customers are saying about you?

A brand is an Agreement.

Who is your current audience? Do you share the same sentiments? What kind of audience do you want to expand into? How will you best communicate your message to your audience?

A brand is your Nature.

It is the intrinsic nature of your message. It is your personality and style. It causes an emotional attachment to your message.

A brand is Distinctive.

It will cause you to stand out among others. It is what makes you unique. It is your identity. It makes others think of you.

When I first started building a brand, the main concentration was on who I would affect?

In the beginning, it was a very delicate area for me. One of my first businesses involved nightlife. I promoted events, and I also owned a DJ company. As a woman who was married at the time and also a mother, I was very conscious about the way I dressed or behaved. Nightlife is a male-dominated industry, so I had to find the balance with my brand to make sure that I fit in the scene but also command respect. As I gained popularity in the music industry, I was also growing in the women empowerment spectrum.

I knew for sure is that not only did my younger mentees follow me but several of my female audiences also had daughters who looked up to me. I had to be cautious with how I acted and cognizant of what I would post. There are times when I enjoy a good ole ratchet post, but I would never put that content on my page. I would side text it to my girlfriends and laugh away. Why would I go that hard? I've heard people say that I'm not being myself or being real. Sometimes people, at first glance, that are introduced to you can see something about you and be turned off. Times have changed so much that your social media is like your business card. I knew that irresponsible posting could negatively affect my brand. I wanted a global business, not a local business.

LILLIE-ISM

"You Are Responsible For How You Act At All Times Regardless Of How You Feel."

I hate talking about my personal life. However, I also understand when God enlarged my territory it would require me getting uncomfortable. Although being vulnerable and transparent in this aspect isn't my strong suit I know it will bring you value.

Here goes an intimate story.
I got to a point in my career where my brand was growing. I received requests for speaking engagements and was

flown to various parts of the country to share my wisdom. As a result, my following continually increased. Every year my kid's father would promote an event called "BEACH-WEAR." I was always in charge of helping with the promotion of the event. On the flyer, you were sure to find scantily clad women. I struggled with this one because I wanted to support him, but I didn't deem that type of promotion appropriate anymore with how I was growing my brand. I opted to invite close friends personally, but I refused to post the flyer.

This situation caused a huge rift in my household; he felt I wasn't supportive. He felt now that I had a larger audience I didn't want to share it with him. I remember crying and feeling I was letting him down. I was so torn, but I knew in my gut it was the right move for me. I had to be rational and think long term. At that moment I decided I had put my brand first. Looking back I would do it a thousand times over.

The result of my decision to protect my brand benefitted my family, especially my children, as they began building their respective businesses. I was very happy my decision also edified me as a respected community leader which benefitted my kid's father on a larger scale.

LILLIE-ISM

"When Your Stock Goes Up So Does Your Behavior."

With all this growth, there is no way I could be seen doing things I did before. You have to allow yourself and your brand to evolve. I come from very humble beginnings. In the streets of NYC people always say they will make it out of the hood. The streets will see someone with a future or potential and say things like, "You have to blow up and make us proud." The crazy part is when you do "make it out the hood" those same people will get mad at you for not doing hood things anymore. Don't fall victim to the horrid disease of ITC (I'm Too Cool). I've witnessed many people throw away opportunity repeatedly to keep their street credibility.

Right now, someone is looking at your grind. Rooms are speaking your name that you haven't walked into yet. Investors are watching your come up and paying attention to your every move. One great play towards your career will cause a major beneficial shift. One bad move will cause that investor to say, "See, we knew she wasn't the one." As unfair as it may seem, the world is majorly critical of women. Do not throw away an amazing opportunity because you didn't understand the importance of branding.

I stand before you as a BAWSE who was able to take her husband's last name and develop it into a huge brand. I was so proud of myself when I received a phone call about one of my annual events. There is a city requesting that I make it a tour and bring my events to them. I am excited about the future where the last name ENNIS becomes an even bigger brand for my children and me all because of the power of branding.

THOU SHALL BUILD A BRAND
WORKSHEET

What makes you feel alive? What values are you grounded in?

What are some words that define your personality?

How do you want people to remember you?

What is a common area that people seek your advice in?

CREATING YOUR BRAND

BRAND MISSION –

BRAND VISION –

BRAND VALUES –

BRAND INTERESTS –

BRAND STRENGTHS –

BRAND WEAKNESSES –

BRAND PERSONALITY –

**The world said: "Be invisible,"
but SHE heard, "Be INVINCIBLE."**

COMMANDMENT FIVE
THOU SHALL NOT BE A HOE

I know I shocked you ladies with this one, right? Well, let's talk! What is a hoe? Typically a hoe is a general insult for a female though can be applied to men also. Most people think a highly promiscuous woman is a whore. In my opinion, a hoe is an attention seeker but for all the wrong reasons. If a woman is sexually engaged and confident in her sex life, to me, doesn't make her a hoe. If she is being responsible, protecting herself and feels empowered, then more power to her. You do however have different categories for hoes.

EXHIBIT A: THE MEDIA HOE

The media hoe is the desperate girl looking for any press or media. She lacks the integrity to be a part of the show. She is found to make up different scenarios to fit into the agenda. For example, if the topic of rape comes up on social media all of a sudden she too is a victim. She has lied about so much that it's challenging to have any empathy. If the topic of racism comes up, she has a video and a hashtag to go along with it. Let us not also forget the fake encounter she had with racism in hopes that her video will go viral. A couple of weeks will pass, and we are talking about a disease. Like a typical hypochondriac, she has a ribbon and a campaign for that as well.

You are laughing, but we all know her. It is disgusting to be on social media, and unfortunately a friend or associate passes away. You know for a fact that the two weren't close yet all of a sudden the clout chasing posts pop up. "OMG, I just spoke to you two days ago, R.I.P. my angel." Can someone bring out the violins already because this person deserves an Oscar! The behavior is ridiculous. Authentic and real will always recognize real.

EXHIBIT B: THE CELEBRITY HOE

The celebrity hoe is a woman who is desperate to prove that she is in the 'Hollywood' circle. She is so out of tune with who she is. Her only way to try and gain credibility and respect is through the efforts, merits, and accolades of others, not hers. These women are often seen at events and will do anything to catch that picture moment with a celebrity to post on social media. The caption typically reads, "Ran into the homie again today."

EXHIBIT C: THE CLOTHING HOE

The clothing hoe is the superficial one focused on the importance of labels. She thinks name brands make her better than other women. She will only value someone based on what they are wearing and not what they are bringing to the table. She doesn't necessarily have a style because her obsession is to throw the labels she owns in people's faces. These women have a $2,000 handbag or $3,000 pair of shoes but won't have a dime in their checking or savings accounts. Sis, I'm here to tell you that is NOT the move.

EXHIBIT D: THE SIDE HOE

The side hoe is a woman that wreaks seeking attention through promiscuity. She is a vixen. This type of woman does anything to get a man even if he belongs to someone else. She is okay with being secretly mistreated as long as she gets what she wants or settles for what she feels she deserves. She is okay with sharing half of a man because she is not a whole woman. This person sees no problem in ruining another Queen because her value system allows her to think it's okay to compete where she doesn't compare. The end goal for her is a man because she doesn't see value in anything else. The only thing she has to give is in between her legs.

EXHIBIT E: THE GOLD DIGGING HOE

The gold digging hoe is the type of woman to puts herself in a financial bind to get floor seats to NBA games or get bottle service at the best club in town so she can flirt with professional athletes or famous artists. Her end goal is to get anything monetary from the relationship.

This type of woman will bypass the good guy who would worship the ground she walks on all because he's not in her preferred tax bracket. What I find hilarious is that she would expect and request a certain income from a partner that she hasn't mastered acquiring for herself.

LILLIE-ISM

"Money Only Impresses Lazy Girls.
When A Woman Works Hard, A Man
With Money Is A Bonus, Not
A Requirement."

I want to talk to you ladies about a huge pet peeve I have. As women in business, we have suffered many challenges of being taken seriously or seen as equals in the workforce. For years, we have fought for fair wages and still must fight off male chauvinism. Here comes this hoe acting like her workplace or her business is www.match.com. I have witnessed women prospect more for their love lives than an opportunity. The sad part is no one wants to have these conversations. No one wants to take a Queen's hand and say, "Hey sis you're better than that. You don't have to do all of this." Women will come into conferences not to develop their inherent talent but rather come like vultures to find the next man with money who can facilitate the lifestyle that they want.

I had a cool acquaintance I met in the networking world. This girl was gorgeous, smart, sharp, super educated, and well to do with a great personality. We were in Vegas at the time and decided to go out for drinks at a popular nightclub. So I got up to get myself a drink, and she stopped me and said, "Give me a minute don't order anything. Let me work the room, and I'll have a bottle sent over to us." I sat back and watched in amazement; it felt like a show. In less than five minutes we had bottle service. I looked forward to us hanging out because she seemed sharp and had a lot going on for her. Several celebrities and athletes rolled in, and I couldn't believe my eyes because she turned into an accountant. She proceeded to tell me their net worth; which one she would or would not date because of their income. I couldn't grasp how she knew this information.

Throughout the night she continued to express that her mother taught her to attend these functions for this matter. Her goal was to snag the right man. She also shared her mother told her to not be a fool like the rest of her cousins who married men without a lot of money or had babies without being wed with nothing to show for it. Her exact words were, "Momma taught me that my womb costs money." I couldn't believe what I was hearing; it was funny and not funny at the same time. Her five-year plan was to find the right man at one of these events because college produced thousandaires, but conferences produced millionaires. Once she found a man worthy of her womb she would get married and pregnant right away so she can stay home and relax. I was shocked at the way she laid out everything and amazed that she worked her entire life to be a gold digger.

LILLIE-ISM

"There Are Certain Things That
Money Cannot Buy; My Vagina Is
One Of Them."

Ladies we have to raise the standard, not only for ourselves but for future generations. We must honor our ancestors that paved the way to greatness. I often wonder are my actions congruent with the generation of women I want to see conquering education, economics, leadership, and sisterhood. You cannot do that by being a hoe.

THOU SHALL NOT BE A HOE

List 10 Things You Can Do To Increase Your Respect Factor

1)

2)

3)

4)

5)

6)

7)

8)

9)

10)

COMMANDMENT SIX
THOU SHALL HAVE YOUR OWN M.B.A

This is one of my favorite topics. Ladies when I say M.B.A., I'm not talking about a master in business administration. You must have your own Money Bank Account. First things first, I know that this is hard. For generations the standard roles were a husband went to work while the woman was the homemaker, there are children and typically one car per family. I'm sure we can all agree that times have changed and drastically. Today's economy requires two incomes coming into a household, especially when everyone needs a car. Why is it women haven't started to protect themselves financially? It is truly a conditioned behavior to have to ask a man for money. I can't imagine having to buy myself lunch or even a pair of underwear and not having an income to do so.

> **LILLIE-ISM**
>
> "There Is No Greater Feeling Than To Purchase Something And Not Have To Ask A Single Soul For Permission."

The more I challenge your mindset on this, the more resistance I will meet. I'm ok with that. We have been programmed to be "sheeple"(foolish followers) and think the same. On this topic, I am okay with standing out like a sore thumb. I am a Christian, and I love the Lord. I have witnessed many women in those demographics being presented with several opportunities whether monetary or career-wise. Many times the response is, "I will have to get back to you. I have to talk it over with my husband." There is something that stirs up strong emotion in me when I hear this. I believe a spouse brings in 100% into the relationship; you should also bring in 100% in the same relationship, and together they become one. It also says in my favorite book that a Proverbs 31 woman is a blessing.

"She is worth far more than rubies.
Her husband has full confidence in her
And lacks nothing in value.
She brings him good, not harm
All the days of her life…
She considers a field and buys it;
Out of her earnings, she plants a vineyard.
She sets about her work vigorously:
Her arms are strong for her tasks.
She sees her trading is profitable,
And her lamp does not go out at night."
Proverbs 31

The good word says all these things about us as women, yet we choose to play a different role, why? I want to feel like a woman, like an equal, like I'm valued and not like a child. I know marriage to be sacred and beautiful covenant, but we have allowed marriage to go from being a relationship to a dictatorship. I'll give you a scenario as an example.

If my place of employment came to me and offered a raise, do you think I should ask for permission to take the raise? No, you should be trusted to make great decisions for yourself and your household. Should the situation arise where you have made a bad decision, then your relationship should be solid and strong enough to have the grace to cover you and get through it.

I have a very close friend, who is an extremely successful accountant. She had all these ideas to purchase properties on how to manage their earnings as a couple. Her husband was a very hard worker and a great provider as a law enforcement officer. She would often come to me because they would often get into financial hardships. I asked "Well aren't you an accountant? It doesn't make sense. You are so sharp." She proceeded to tell me that although she is an accountant and her profession deals with finances, all decision making is done by him. My heart was crushed and hearing this blew my mind because I hated to see my friends in such a bind because of how their household was governed. My mom always taught me to stay out of married folks business, so I didn't say much. They had a joint account, and she didn't have a personal account. As time went by she had to sit and watch him make one bad decision after another.

That level of misogyny has to change. You have to call a spade a spade. I cannot tell you how many times financial institutions or advisors will still call a house and ask for your husband even though YOU answered the phone. This is not okay. According to financial publications, more than half of the women in America defer to their spouse on investment decisions and financial planning. Why? An IRA stands for Individual Retirement Account for crying out loud.

LILLIE-ISM

"Investing In Yourself Will Be Your Greatest Investment."

The reason why women are going this route starts at home. Parents this will be a necessary eye-opener. In a home where there are children of both genders, there are talks with sons about risk-taking, wealth, and how to grow wealth. The talks that will take place with daughters is typically about playing it safe, saving money, and having fiscal responsibility. Furthermore, they will pay their sons more money than their daughters for doing the same chores. It is preposterous and to think this first example is starting at home. Then we wonder why there is such difficulty to break this methodology. The habit of encouraging old gender roles puts both the sons and daughters on different trajectories within their financial map.

If you are married or in a committed long term relationship, I wish your love years of success. Ladies you should adore, love, and honor your spouse but you shouldn't be stupid.

I shared an amazing opportunity with a colleague five years ago. Although she was super excited about it and wanted to partake her husband said no. I remember being a little disappointed because it just wasn't what I was used to. You are the mindset of the five people you speak to most, and I learned to start keeping great company. I kept company with people who had the lifestyles I desired. A close friend and mentor of mine Valerie Acosta was known for having her husband sleep on the couch when he wasn't happy about one of her business ventures. Now, together they have cleared multiple millions in revenue. Chile sometimes you have to deny him the cookie if you follow my drift- wink wink.

Nonetheless, this amazing lady followed what she felt was the right thing to do, listened to her husband and declined the opportunity. I received an urgent phone call from her just a couple of weeks ago. She stated that she would like to shadow me for a day and that she wanted to go into business for herself. Of course I was so excited to hear this new development in her life; however, she turned to me and started crying. I was confused. She explained that she felt very sorry and guilty for distancing herself from me over the past couple of years. She told me how desperately she needed to go into business for herself and make this work. Her husband had left her, she had no money, and he also took the house in the divorce. Life hit her hard, and she regretted not working with me years ago. I hugged her tightly, told her it's ok, and this is part of her journey. It is better for her to learn now rather than later and waste more years. There is nothing wrong with loving your spouse but God forbid they decide to up and leave you should have your bag secured.

LILLIE-ISM

"Go Against Everything, Especially If It Means Following Your Gut!"

When working on getting your own money, your attitude toward money counts. I'm very blessed to have an amazing church with a phenomenal and strong pastor. She tends to change my perspective on several things. One of the best lessons I learned from her is that if God is God, He cannot be replaced by other things. So if your issue with money is that you are in debt, you cannot turn around and make debt your god. "Money is a spirit, and sometimes it gets offended at what you spend it on, and that's why you don't have any." –Pastor Cynthia G. West

If all you do is talk about debt, then you are making your problem and your debt your god. You are subconsciously making them bigger than your God. Since I heard that message, I stopped complaining about paying my bills. I started to praise God for the provision He has granted and the ability to pay those bills.

It was important for me to start owning my buying power. If I wanted to not only make my money but attract more money to me, I needed to change how I perceived and spoke about it. I don't spend money, I don't pay bills, and I circulate money into the economy and my community. The electric company needs my bill money to stay in business; the gas company needs me to stay in business. I support my dentists business by bringing my business there. I wear reading glasses. They happen to be Valentino who is a really big designer. However, my mindset is fixed on the fact I am doing Valentino a favor by bringing them business. That transaction shifted how I look at all future transactions.

LILLIE-ISM

"Don't Hold Onto Crumbs – A Closed Fist Can Never Open Up To Receive Bread."

It is important that once you make money and have developed a good attitude about money, you start to spread the wealth. Once you have your own M.B.A. you will start to become a money magnet. At that point wealth and abundance will be attracted to you. Once you start living in that abundance, it is very important that you sow seeds with a good attitude.

I cannot stress how blessed you will be when you support other women in business. I also have a disclaimer that comes with that statement. If you want blessings to come your way, you must sow seeds with your own money. Once you start supporting other women, the laws of attraction demand whatever you do or focus on to expand.

THOU SHALL HAVE YOUR OWN
M.B.A. WORKSHEET

"America's daughters are just as capable of defending liberty as her sons." – Senator Tammy Duckworth

Money is as much about the wallet as it is about the mind. List five things you fear about money and what actions you will take to overcome them.

1)

2)

3)

4)

5)

If you have a social media calendar, you should have a financial calendar. Are there any huge financial expenses you need to take on and budget for this year?

JANUARY	FEBRUARY	MARCH	APRIL
MAY	JUNE	JULY	AUGUST
SEPTEMBER	OCTOBER	NOVEMBER	DECEMBER

"Make your own money so that a man has nothing to offer you but loyalty."

COMMANDMENT SEVEN
THOU SHALL BE YOUR
KIDS FIRST HERO

I am the proud mommy of two boys. My oldest son, Omar Ennis aka DJ Bam Bam, is fifteen years old. He began dee-jaying at the tender age of two. I always knew he had a musical gift because as a toddler he would turn over baby wipe boxes to make rhythm and beats on them. Since then Omar has flourished into an amazing scholar and teenpre-neur. Aside from being a DJ, he is a music producer, audio and video engineer, and owner of his company called AMP (A Master Plan). AMP encompasses the three main pillars of his life which are athletics, music, and power. I am so proud of Omar, and he hasn't scratched the surface of what he will accomplish.

My youngest son, Landon Ennis aka Lando Kicks, is nine years old. He is a super intelligent and funny boy that lives for basketball. He has a passion for dancing and rapping. He just dropped his first single on iTunes, released on his brother's music label. I am equally excited to see him grow even more into his purpose.

Many people have complimented me on my children and asked what my biggest parenting tip is. My response is always the same, be the best possible YOU. Remember, you are your children's first teacher and their best example. I've heard so many parents say to their children, "When you grow up I want you to be better than me." That is nearly impossible if you aren't setting the bar high yourself.

LILLIE-ISM

"I've Never Wanted To Put A Lid On My Children's Success, Which Is Why Every Chance I Get, I Go Harder."

Not because I prefer to be busy, but I want to provide my children with the best advantages possible. I also want to show them what they are capable of. If I fall short on my work ethic then what example is that for my children? Your kids will not follow what you say, but they will do what you do.

LILLIE-ISM

"You Cannot Motivate Your Kids By Preaching To Them About What's Good For Them, But You Can Inspire Them Through Your Actions."

When Landon was a toddler, he often picked up books and read them. Every morning I would wait for my oldest to go to school. That was my "me" time where I would curl up with a book. I would relax on my favorite sofa, lay on my back and my legs crossed up in the air. Sure enough, Landon would wake up shortly after and I would catch him lying right next to me in the same position. It cracked me up.

As he moved into school age, I realized his love for reading had dissipated as he got older. One day I asked him why he doesn't read anymore. I found myself constantly harassing him to read, and he would give me a hard time. Landon has a very witty, smart mouth and replied, "Well, I don't see you reading so why should I?"

Although I read in the mornings, Landon was at school during that time. I had to adjust my schedule and start reading when he came home from school so he could physically see me reading. It was important for him to have a visual to model that same behavior.

Many have also asked about Omar and how is he so talented at such a young age. The answer is simple; his Dad is super talented. As parents, we've heard the craziest things about Omar and how we raised him. They thought because his Dad is a DJ, we were hard on him and forced him to become one. People thought Oraine ran drills with him at home. It's hilarious the things we have heard. When I was working in the hospital, Omar spent the bulk of his days with his Dad. He heard him in the house working on music all the time. He saw him making flyers for his graphics company; he would also accompany Oraine to many gigs. His Dad always kept a pair of turntables in the house and Omar would jump on them daily.

One day as he accompanied his Dad to a gig and there was an issue setting up the sound system. They'd done the task several times successfully, but they had trouble that day. His Dad was stumped trying to figure it out when Omar, who was two years old at the time, walked over to the speakers, amplifiers, and simply switched some wires around troubleshooting the issue. We all stood astonished. It was right there, and then I knew we had to continue to work hard to lead by example. From that day forward as a family, we've continuously challenged each other to rise to higher heights.

There is a certain level of awareness and type of mind-set needed when parenting. If you are constantly saying and declaring things that you don't want to appear in your children's lives, then stop saying it out loud. If you hang around with five broke people, not only are you bound to be the sixth but who will your children have as an example for success that they know on a personal level? All of my close friends clear at least six figures annually. What used to be a ceiling for me goal-wise is now a floor for my children. I remember thinking to myself I have to find a good job to make that kind of money. Because of their surroundings and the conversations my boys hear around them, they know the bare minimum of what they should be working toward is clearing six figures.

Teach your children to be courageous and individual. Going against the grain is okay. Some people will attack your livelihood, but you must always stand up for yourself. I recall one time I walked into the barbershop to drop my son for a haircut. There was a guy I knew of and knew he was publicly bashing my travel company. When I walked in he said, "Oh there she goes, it's Miss Hollywood. I'm surprised you're here and not on another vacation haha. You trying to come into the barbershop to scam more people for your pyramid?" I promptly replied, "Funny I've never run into you at the airport. Do you have at least one stamp on your passport?

I didn't think so because people who watch other people's lives from home seldom have anything going on themselves. Life isn't a spectator sport you should get up and do something instead of watching." Ohhhhhh he got big mad. He said you didn't have to go there and get disrespectful. I said, "You didn't need to have your nose in my business but you did, and since you walked right into that one, let me escort you right out with this. I do not rob or steal from anyone; I provide value. I make an honorable living, so the next time you think you can attack my livelihood without me defending how I feed my children, think again."

Several times, people attacked our DJ business combined with our parenting. People disapproved of my son listening to music with explicit lyrics. Please also had issues with us having our boys up late night at concerts opening up for other artists. What I didn't know is Omar was being mocked at school and children were telling him he was a fake DJ. I know now because he witnessed me defending our family and businesses; he opened up to us about what was happening at school. We were happy to hear that he addressed it and with confidence defended himself just the same.

> ## LILLIE-ISM
>
> "If You Don't Teach Your Children The Value System You Want Them To Know, They Will Learn Someone Else's By Default."

Teaching my children they have value is the best thing I have done so far. They are my business partners, and I constantly ask them for their feedback. I assign them titles and responsibilities to go along with those titles. I always want them to have a sense of ownership in what I am doing. The worst thing you can do is create a culture where success and edification isn't the norm. Landon used to struggle sometimes in our family. He would see his mommy, daddy, and brother all with businesses and making money. He wanted to not only make money but feel valued and useful in our family dynamics. His Dad started assigning him the tasks of carrying specific DJ equipment, and at the end of the gig, he would get paid.

Omar has a very calm demeanor, and Landon is the firecracker. In my line of business, I typically have to be in front of the room doing presentations. It is a very quiet environment which isn't conducive to a fiery child. I didn't want to be that busy mom that gave a tablet or phone to her kids and neglected them. I also didn't want to be the mom that let her kids run crazy in a business setting. I can't believe it worked, but I figured out another option. I thought outside the box and told my baby that he is my Executive Director. I told Landon that my slideshow had 49 slides in it and that I needed him to help me count my slides while I was presenting to ensure that I had exactly 49 and not one slide over.

I would crack up in the middle of the presentation just looking at my baby as he took his tiny notebook out of his book bag and concentrate as he marked up the sheet as I clicked a slide to keep count. I would greet him with so much enthusiasm and tell him that I'm so thankful he came out to help me because I couldn't imagine doing all of this without him. He walked around feeling so important.

Of course, as he got older that trick didn't work anymore, so I started bringing a timer with me. I would ask him to time my presentations and make sure that I would speak under 35 minutes. I became creative about him helping me, and then he naturally started stepping up on his own without being asked. He became such an efficient child that he grew into being a huge asset to his brothers' company and now holds the title of CFO. The blessing in all of this is that I'm raising two sharp and confident kidpreneurs. Also, as parents, their Dad and I get to duplicate the things we love about ourselves into them.

THOU SHALL BE YOUR KID'S FIRST HERO WORKSHEET

**"You're never too old to start,
but you're never too young to start either."**

What are three things your child organically loves to do?

●

●

●

What are three strengths they have? (Never focus on a child's weakness, build up their strengths)

●

●

●

What are three ways you can support them as the parent?

●

●

●

What are three ways you can lead by example?

●

●

●

"Tomorrow's future begins today."

COMMANDMENT EIGHT
THOU SHALL EMBRACE
YOUR SEASONS

There are two things that I jokingly say are guaranteed to happen in life. One of them is bills, and the other is a challenge. There are ebbs and flows, as well as, peaks and valleys. Life has its seasons. I live in the great state of Connecticut and whether it is for business or other reasons I am constantly being asked to move to a major city. Several people have inquired about why my big personality chooses to stay in such a small state. A huge part of why I love living in CT and don't want to move is because I get to experience all four seasons. Life can be the same full of different seasons. If you don't learn to appreciate and embrace your seasons, life can become pretty mundane.

My favorite season is autumn. There is something about the joy of school back in session, the smell in the air, the thought of pumpkin, apple, spice and everything nice. The holidays of Halloween and Thanksgiving bring about a very warm and fuzzy feeling. I enjoy the layering of clothes and the super cute fall fashion. My whole attitude around the fall changes, I know that Christmas is right around the corner and the weather is simply delightful.

One day I was sitting down with my grandpa watching him rake up the leaves. I was telling him how beautiful they were and that he should leave them on the lawn and let them blow everywhere. His response, "Why would I let something dead just fly around." He said that in the summer the grass is green and the trees are full. When autumn comes, it's as if people forget that when the leaves are changing from green to red, yellow, and orange, it is because they are dying.

The reason they call autumn fall is because that's exactly what leaves do when they die. I thought to myself, 'wow a dark season can still be beautiful.' What I love about this is after fall and winter come spring. Meaning, after darkness, there will always be light. After darkness, there is always a re-birth, a re-launch. If you are currently going through something heavy and dark know that something beautiful is being birthed out of this.

I want you to stop reading right now and think of a moment where you went through something so painful you thought it would ruin and finish you. However, you came out of it. Whatever current obstacle you are facing, you need to take 15 seconds and clap for yourself. Sometimes you need to praise God in advance for what He is about to do in your life.

LILLIE-ISM

"God Greatest Creation Is Birthed In Darkness For Nine Months Before It Sees The Light."

A baby has to grow and nurture in a dark place before it is birthed. A butterfly doesn't spread its wings to fly until it has conquered its cocoon phase. Even my favorite scripture says that weeping may endure for a night, but joy comes in the morning. A huge mistake I have seen firsthand is when people quit right before the season has a chance to change. A great friend of mine has a saying that helps me in moments like this. "You're not being picked on, you've been picked." –Derron Walker

Every time I thought life was working against me, there was a miracle around the corner. At the age of four, my parents got a divorce. What I didn't understand in that season was the divorce led to me learning to be independent. There were times where I had to cook meals for myself or do chores before my mom got home from school or work. This circumstance gave me a tremendous set of life skills that I would need later in life. It also made me a great time manager.

An injury to the knee made me fall in love with rehabilitative medicine which also brought me to the great state of Connecticut by way of Sacred Heart University. The university is where I met my children's father, and I wouldn't have my two amazing sons had he not come into my life.

As a professional working in the hospital, fighting cancer gave me a better appreciation to seize every day. I learned to take full advantage of every living moment. Losing my job shortly after taught me to keep an open mind on the different ways to accrue income. My children's father instilled in me the spirit of entrepreneurship, and I was able to make a total career change post Breast Cancer. I went through a very humbling season after losing my job and being unemployed for three years led to my house going into pre-foreclosure. It taught me to save more and be more fiscally responsible. There were a lot of material things in my closet that couldn't pay my bills, and I needed to change that.

LILLIE-ISM

"Stop Having Items In Your Closet Valued More Than What Is In Your Savings. Clothes Cannot Pay Your Bills!"

I was able to get creative. I was so desperate to make money and put food on the table, I went door to door for an energy company. All I received were doors slammed in my face. I'm so thankful for those moments because those doors slammed in my face and being hung up on gave me the tenacity and the resiliency I needed in business later down the line.

I started a company called Libra and before I could make sure everything was legit I sold liquor out of the back of my trunk. During these sales, I had no idea that selling liquor without permits was illegal. Let's say favor was on my side that I didn't get caught in the process. I began educating myself on all the business laws. Nonetheless, I learned about the grind and hustle, to walk in fearlessness without the worry of failing. Matter of fact, I fail forward. It also showed me that I was built for this. Nothing but God would've stopped me.

During my time of humility, I thought God was punishing me, but He was pushing me towards my purpose. I would get tired of people calling me nonstop and asking me for referrals or advice. I realized that my annoyance was my anointing and so I started The Lillie Ennis Group.

Just when I thought I could make it through anything that life brought on, I reached the biggest heartbreaking obstacle of them all. This major pain affected my career, my public image, my life, and my household. I had no choice but to embrace this season because I just knew God was working something out on my behalf. I also knew that I couldn't serve two masters. My options were either I served faith, or I served fear, and I chose to serve faith.

My deepest darkest moment was when my husband whom I loved very much had a very public affair. It was on tabloid websites and all over social media. I was the talk of the town, and shamed. It baffles me how people will talk so much junk about the wife who was cheated on.

I said to myself there is no way that I am having P Diddy and J Lo problems without having P Diddy and J Lo money. I was gaining a lot of popularity in the women empowerment section. I was responsible for mentoring many girls and women entrepreneurs. All the lights were on me.

He had a major event coming up, and everyone was wondering whether I would still show up or not. I chose to play a Hillary Clinton and attend the event with all smiles though hell was brewing at home.

One thing about me, I am about my coins. I knew that if I didn't show up that people would talk about the situation more and would also try and pick sides. If they were Team Lillie, then most likely they wouldn't support his events for a while. But guess what? The result would be a win for me but a loss for Omar and Landon. One thing I could never take away from their Dad is that he is an amazing provider and an awesome father. Many women fail to realize emotions get you nowhere; you have to be smart. The problem is when the light is shining on you, it's shining on the good and bad. You must be prepared for both.

I remember being embarrassed and everyone waiting for me to respond or react to this horrible situation. I refused! I even lost people who I thought were my friends in this situation. I had people trying to perpetrate as my friends to get details out of me. I had people unfollow me on social media because I refused to address the issue. They said I was being fake and acting like my life was perfect. I knew it was far from perfect, but I also knew what not to give my attention. I also knew how to buy a journal instead of treating Facebook like one.

Now hear me out ladies as much as I wanted to be a woman scorned and turn up and be ratchet, I'm lucky I had some real women around me that wouldn't let me show my you know what. I embraced the season because I understood that God was working all things out for my good. What God allowed to happen blessed me. All it did was promote me. I'm down with O.P.P. (Obstacles and Problems Promote). I'm so thankful that God enlarged my territory. Had my life been so peachy perfect or so cookie cutter the way I wanted it to be, I wouldn't be in the position I am today. I wouldn't be able to minister to women on a higher plane.

LILLIE-ISM

"What You Go Through Is Never For You. It's Always To Help Someone Else Get Through In The Future."

I'm in a very special place in life where I find comfort in the seasons. I see beauty in every one of them. I know that when that next obstacle or hurdle comes, I will give a little wink to God, standing in obedience and patience for what He will do on my behalf.

THOU SHALL EMBRACE
YOUR SEASONS WORKSHEET

What are three of your darkest moments?

-
-
-

What did you learn from those situations?

-
-
-

How did those situations impact you in this season?

-
-
-

COMMANDMENT NINE
THOU SHALL AWAKEN
THE BEAST IN YOU

Often women will ask me how I can get so many men to respect me not only personally but also in business. The answer is quite funny, but it's the truth. I'M A BEAST! My aura, my position, my posture, and my demeanor all affirm that I am nothing to play with. I have had this attitude since I was a little girl. My Dad was my world; I was such a daddy's girl. I was laughing hanging out with my dad one day, and he was telling me that as a child he would introduce me to his friends. If for some reason I didn't care for them I wouldn't say hello. My dad would threaten me to say hello, or I would be punished or spanked. No matter what he threatened me with, I wouldn't budge.

My dad always prepared me to be tough, but he was also loving and caring toward me. He instilled a lot of confidence in me. He would say, "Pollo" yes that translates to chicken in Spanish but it is my dad's term of endearment for me. "Pollo, anything the guys do you can do too. Don't be afraid mama." Having my Daddy come to my games always gave me an extra boost of confidence. He is also the reason for my competitive spirit.

One of my favorite pastimes was Saturday mornings where we would ride bikes to Mullaly Park in the Bronx and then race on the track. He would also take me to the bowling alley right across the street from Yankee Stadium where I would spend hours trying to beat him. Fast forward, having that time with my dad resulted in me being the only female bowler, not only in Cardinal Spellman High School, but the entire division.

Now let's bring it back to my mom, Big Lil. She is where I get my posture. Everyone that comes across her can't believe how big of a person she is despite stature. This less than five-foot beauty will walk right up to you with a firm handshake and look you straight in the eye and say, "Hi, my name is Big Lil." Thank God for my amazing parents because they were the perfect combination of teaching me that I have no limits.

LILLIE-ISM

"Even When You Think I'm Silent,
Trust There Is Thunder Inside Of Me."

If there is ever a time where a woman forgets how powerful she is, I remind her to take a look at the animal kingdom. The reason we have been conditioned to be meek and kind is because everyone knows the power of a woman. After all, we are responsible for bringing in life. The future is female ladies, and we should start to own that.

LILLIE-ISM

"Society Forgets That It's
The Lioness Who Hunts."

Yes, the Lion is the king of the jungle who is respected and feared. The lion is also a big sleeper. He is up for a few hours in the day and serves by standing guard and protecting the pride from trespassers. The lioness, on the other hand, goes out daily and hunts to feed their family.

The Queen Bee is another great example. I was watching an animal show where they were showing a beehive was under attack. Not one single bee left until the Queen Bee gave the command to move, and then, everyone else followed. I was fascinated by that notion and realized the same spirit lived in me. There is nothing wrong with being confident, competitive, and assertive. The world needs more women like that.

LILLIE-ISM

"Strong Women – May We Be Them,
May We Know Them And May We
Raise Them."

I remember going through some growing pains in my business. This specific business venture I started with three of my closest friends; Marlon, Warren, and Smooth. I was in a serious dilemma where I wasn't sure what to do. I spoke to them, and I explained the pros and cons of each decision I was contemplating. Smooth stands up passionately and says, "Whatever you say is what we will follow. You are my leader, and I trust you. Whatever you do I'm behind you 100%." I think about that often, and I usually get choked up. These men are tough guys, principally Smooth. He is not very trusting of others. He is also older than me. The fact that I had his full vote of confidence is something I will never forget.

It is one thing as a woman to lead other women. However, leading other men as a woman is a gift. I am forever grateful to God for giving me that character to be able to lead in life and awaken that inner animal instinct that is hiding in every single one of us.

LILLIE-ISM

"I Won Because I'm Not Afraid Of Losing And I Am Not Afraid Of Leading."

THOU SHALL AWAKEN THE INNER BEAST IN YOU WORKSHEET

"Leadership belongs to she who takes it."

Name three women in your life that inspire you to level up:

-
-
-

COMMANDMENT TEN
THOU SHALL CELEBRATE
OTHER WOMEN

I mentioned in an earlier chapter that women have a habit of comparing. We are categorized about one another as being catty, petty, and outright mean. You see it on social media daily, "Oh such and such hates on me." This narrative is upsetting because I despise when women don't get along.

Allow me to make something very clear. I am no angel. Many moons ago I used to be the queen of shade. I had a very smart mouth, and my clap backs were loaded. Legitimately, I was the Queen of smart remarks. I was also the person where you didn't have to do anything for me to dislike you. If you rubbed me the wrong way, I didn't like you. I used to be ashamed to admit this, but then I realized you could never deliver people from what you never came out of.

As women, we can be salty and refuse to share our crowns with other Queens. Well hater, my question to you is on a scale from pretzel to ocean how salty are you? What women fail to realize is that God will often unlock someone else's blessings before He unlocks yours, to see if you are happy for them. You should always celebrate women regardless of religion, race, creed, or socioeconomic background.

Why? We all face the same battles. You should be embracing and uplifting one another. Women together make the vision possible.

LILLIE-ISM

"Behind Every Successful Woman Is A Tribe Of Women That Have Her Back."

One of my greatest friendships came from a messy situation. March is Women's History Month, and I have always thrown events in that month to celebrate women. One of my biggest annual events is called The Big Hat Brunch. Rumors were flying around that a lady I didn't know at the time, named Shantana didn't like me. She was saying that I was trying to copy her by throwing women events in March, which is also Endometriosis Awareness Month. She is the founder of a wonderful organization called the Sistergirl Foundation that provides advocacy for women's health issues.

When I found out about the luncheon she was hosting, I decided to purchase a ticket and meet her for myself. When I arrived, she instantly embraced me. I loved the whole energy of that event. Would you know she heard the same rumor of me talking about her? We laughed about this scenario the entire time and connected in a very powerful way. We became very close friends, and I now have the esteemed privilege of being on her board. She hosted my next event, and we've worn crowns ever since. She has been such a blessing to my life. I'm thankful that someone started those rumors.

There is another story of friendship that came into my life. The situation could've gone very well or very bad. I'm glad it went well. As I began one of my businesses, I was off to a speedy start. I was breaking records in the company and doing great things. A gentleman I was working closely with at the time said I need you to meet Tarah Davis. When I met her in person, she pushed me to do something I did not want to do, but I listened. She's been bossing me around ever since. No, I'm kidding, but I was very open to being coachable. Although I didn't know her as well, she had the lifestyle I wanted. My momma raised no fool. As I was getting closer to breaking another record she called me and was so excited. She offered her help, but her exact words were. "I want to help you surpass my rank." Let's be clear! You do not find that type of mentality in business or among women often. I knew from that moment she was a keeper.

These women among many other family members and friends have been amazing. I have been so blessed to know as many wonderful powerhouses as I do. My women tribe is insane. I can truly say that I am blessed by the caliber of women that I know.

We owe it to our ancestors to celebrate other women. I thank God for the Madame CJ Walker's, Susan B. Anthony's, Rita Moreno's, and the Oprah's that have paved the way for women today to have the rights we deserve and enjoy. When we honor and praise the women that came before us, we don't allow their struggle to be in vain. One of my favorite lines from one of my all-time best poets is this:

"I come as one, but I stand as 10,000" - **Maya Angelou**

So many of us are working hard, but we must always remember if we get the opportunity to crash the glass ceiling we have a duty and obligation to send that elevator back down.

I hosted a networking event and all the entrepreneurs in the room were going around and introducing them-selves, saying their name and the current projects they were working on. There was this gorgeous young lady that start-ed speaking. All I could do is think about how amazing she is. In my head, I couldn't wait to connect with her and compliment what she was working on.

As the event ended she approached me. I smiled and hugged her, and she was shocked. She mentioned she had been following me for a while and admired my work for quite some time.

She then mentioned that she modeled a lot of what she was doing from watching me. Flattered, my heart was elated, and I jumped right in and started giving her some pointers. She proceeded to tell me that a couple of women she spoke to about her projects were not supportive. Better yet she said that some of them downplayed it saying that her projects have been done before - tsk tsk tsk. I proceeded to tell her that they were dumb and a bunch of haters. DISCLAIMER! I am a straight shooter. I tell it like it is, like it or leave it. I continued to encourage her. I told her even if what they said was true, is it safe to say that young women in our community still have a demand for help? Yes or yes? She replied, "Yes!" I said then your work is not done. Continue to be great!

As an OG in the game, you have to check yourself and pass the baton. Learn how to collaborate and congratulate. Don't be that woman that forgets to share her crown or extend a hand or platform for an up and coming Queen. One of my mentors Lucinda Cross has looked out for me since the day I met her. It is your responsibility to nurture and cultivate women. If you see a female entrepreneur, support her business. I can't tell you the number of things I have purchased that I had no true desire for. But because I wanted to support my fellow Queen I did. Every time I support it feels great to do so. Heal from past hurts and learn to love on other women, so we don't have to continue to pass down this misguided culture. We are strong! Women who love and women who are creating the next group of strong women that will lead the world.

THOU SHALL CELEBRATE
OTHER WOMEN WORKSHEET

List the women who paved the way for you and find a way
to thank them.

-
-
-
-
-
-
-
-
-
-
-
-
-
-
-
-

CONCLUSION

There you have it, The 10 Glam Commandments. Life happens, but it is how you respond to it. We are in an ever learning space as we walk the earth. Stay open-minded, focused, support other women, and always maintain your glam.

Lovingly,
Lillie, Your Big Sister

ABOUT THE AUTHOR

Lillie Ennis was born and raised in the Bronx, NY. She currently resides with her two sons Omar Ennis and Landon Ennis in Trumbull, CT. Lillie Ennis has earned her degrees in Healthcare and has served as the clinical coordinator for Wellness and Rehabilitation programs in CT hospitals for several years.

Since then Lillie Ennis has become the founder of The Lillie Ennis Group; a networking and consulting firm geared towards highlighting local businesses as well as mentoring clients towards personal and professional enhancement. She is co-owner of Sibling Music LLC; an entertainment company she runs with Oraine Ennis. Lillie also takes great pride in serving as "momager" to her fifteen yearold son DJ BamBam "your featured presentation" and nine year old Lando Kicks the rap god. Lillie likes to stay busy; she is currently working on several projects launching this year.

Lillie has dedicated her life's work to philanthropic causes. She is an esteemed Board Member of the Junior Women's Club of Fairfield. She is passionate about helping her community as she is also the Vice President for Alpha Community Shelter Services where they organize the annual walk to end homelessness in Connecticut. She sits on several boards and committees that are responsible for providing grants and scholarships to young women. Lillie coordinates several fundraising and community events such as the Hoop Dream Charity Birthday Bash to combat childhood hunger, The Breast Cancer Awareness Walk in Bridgeport, CT, as well as being responsible for building a DreamCourt in Bridgeport, CT.

Lillie was diagnosed with Breast Cancer in April 2007 and is proud to say that "she kicked cancer's ass" She is blessed to be in her eleventh year of being a "Conqueror." Lillie is a huge advocate for women empowerment. Lillie is a lover of life and is known for her mantra, "I'd rather be exhausted by success than rested by mediocrity." She volunteers at the Norma Pfriem Breast Cancer Center to help provide holistic resources to post-cancer patients.

Lillie is a serial entrepreneur. She is a top income earner with her travel and lifestyle company. She is often found traveling all over the world to share her testimony with motivational speeches.